Curtis DuRant

BELIZE

The Official Travel Guide

Table of Contents

Introduction

Welcome and thank you so much for purchasing *Belize: The Official Travel Guide!*

Whether you are trying to decide on a location for your next getaway or enjoy learning more about new countries, be prepared for the chapters of this book to whisk you away to an exotic piece of land right off the Caribbean Sea. I assure you that this country will make it to a spot on your bucket list of destinations.

Within the following chapters, you will find all you need to know about the country of Belize. From geography and weather to entertainment and renowned Belize locations, you will get to know this small in size but large in attraction country like the back of your hand!

Thanks again for choosing to purchase this travel guide of the country of Belize! I hope that you find all of the information you are looking for and are even convinced to book a trip to this easily charming country! Every effort was made to ensure it is full of as much useful information as possible, please enjoy!

Chapter 1
A Brief Look at Belize

If you are currently on the hunt for somewhere on Earth to get away from the stressful hustle and bustle of everyday life, perhaps you should veer towards a destination that strives for tranquility. I want to welcome you to the small, Central American country of Belize; a paradise all its own, nicely tucked away with amazing experiences and once-in-a-lifetime views you will want to die for.

Where is Belize?

Belize is located in southern Mexico, right in the heart of the Caribbean Basin. To the east, you can capture wild views of the Caribbean Sea, and to the west, you will find Guatemala.

The History of Belize

The first developers who were responsible for establishing this country were the Mayans around the year 1500 B.C.E. The Maya created quite a number of settlements in Belize during their time. In fact, in the heart of the Belize jungles, you can find the ancient Mayan ruins.

The Mayans had a strong hold over this piece of land until Mr. Christopher Columbus met with the coast of Belize in 1502.

It wasn't until 1638 that England established Belize as a European settlement, which is whose jurisdiction it was under for more than 150 years. Belize became a "Colony of British Honduras" in 1840, becoming a crown colony in 1862. For over 100 years, Belize played the role of a representative government of England.

In 1964, a full self-government paired with a ministerial system was granted, and in 1973 the name changed from British Honduras to Belize. By 1981, Belize gained its full independence.

Belize used to be one of the biggest banana and sugar producers on the planet, but since the prices have dropped way down, poverty in these areas of production began to take hold. Their main industry is oil and tourism.

The network of lagoons, creeks, and rivers throughout Belize have played a major role in the overall historical geography of this country. One of the most historically documented rivers is the Belize River, which is responsible for draining more than a quarter of the country, winding through the edge of the Maya Mountains and crossing the center of the country near Belize City.

Also referred to as Old River, the Belize River served as a direction navigational route throughout the Guatemalan border and was used as the main avenue of communication between the interior land and the coastline. All of the river valleys that make up Belize possess fertile soils that have supported the cultivation of human civilizations for hundreds of years.

Chapter 2
Geography

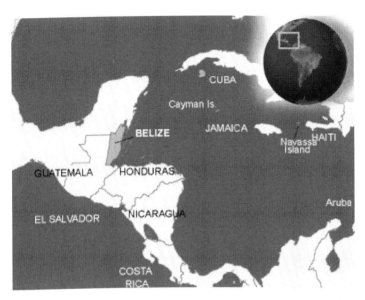

Belize is a small Central American country that is bordered by the Caribbean Sea, Mexico, and Guatemala. The mainland is around 180 miles in length and 68 miles in width. While Belize is only 8,800 square miles in size, it's population as of the end of 2017 is nearing 388,000. This may seem like quite a lot of folks taking up the eccentric beach scenery, but Belize is action the least dense in population compared to the rest of Central America.

Located right against the Caribbean coast, Belize is blessed to be able to share in the territory of the second biggest barrier reef in the world, which flanks a massive 240 miles. To put the size of Belize into perspective, it is just slightly bigger than the state if New Jersey. With the many lagoons that sprinkle the coastlines, the actual land area of this country is only about 8,300 square miles.

Population

Regarding population, Belize has the highest growth rate at 1.87% per year, which is the highest in the entire Western Hemisphere. This alone should speak for itself about the country!

Landscape

The country of Belize is split into four geographic regions:

1. Maya Mountains: located in the southern region and dominate the majority of the coastal plain

2. Northern lowlands: made up of streams and rivers

3. Flat and swampy coastal plain

4. Caribbean coastline: made up of lagoons, islands, and cayes

The Maya Mountains, located in the southern portion of Belize, are surrounded by plateaus and basins that take over much of the coastal plain. It is a low mountain range, only extending to about 1,100 feet in height, with the highest point at 1,124 meters, which is referred to as

Doyle's Delight. This area is sprinkled with highly erodible soils that are not high in fertility, which makes these heavily forested highlands hardly inhabited.

The other part of the Belize region is scattered with 18 rivers and streams that are responsible for draining out the water from low-lying areas. This is what makes the coastlines, especially on the southern side of Belize, so swampy.

List of Belize Islands

If the country of Belize wasn't gorgeously sustaining enough, there are a plethora of tiny islands that scatter the Caribbean coastline:

- Silk Caye

- Glover's Reef Atoll

- South Water Caye

- Goff's Caye

- St. George's Caye

- Tobacco Caye

- Laughing Bird Caye

- Half Mood Caye

- Caye Caulker

- Ambergris Caye

A Network of Rivers and Forestry

The Hondo and Sarstoon Rivers are what defines the northern and southern boundaries on Belize, with the western portion of the border following no natural features as it runs both north and south through the forest lowlands.

Thanks to the rugged geography of the Belize coastlines, it attracts drug smugglers as well as those who wish to get into Mexico. This happens too much that back in 2011 Belize was listed by the United States as one of the main nations to consider for drug producers as well as a place for transit for narcotics to other countries.

Biodiversity

Belize is extremely rich with an array of wildlife thanks to its exclusive place between North and South America. It is home to a great range of both animal and plant life.

Despite the seemingly high number in population, Belize has many miles of land that are untouched, making it a superb location for over 5,000 species of plants and many hundreds of species of animals, like monkeys, snakes, and armadillos, just to name a select few.

Even though that much of the wildlife is greatly preserved in the Belize area, there is a sanctuary known as Cockscomb Basin Wildlife Sanctuary that is in south-central Belize. It was established to provide protection to the forests, watersheds, and fauna. Founded in 1990, it was the first sanctuary that harbored jaguars, and it has been regarded to be one of the best sites of jaguar preservation in the entire world.

Despite the small area of land that Belize covers, this country offers a broad array of wildlife as well as habitats. The lowlands and savannas are home to the rarest of waterfowl, while the forest inhabits tropical birds, tapirs, and pumas, with the mountainous areas being a prosperous niche for outstanding wildcats.

There are 145 species of mammals that currently reside in Belize, with 139 reptiles and amphibian species, more than 56 of those being snakes. With the tropical weather, more than 500 species of rare exotic birds inhabit the country. Thanks to the conservation efforts that are in place in Belize, both citizens and tourists alike can enjoy this broad variety of animal species.

Big Cats

- **Jaguars** are one of the largest of the Central American carnivores. Jaguars are nocturnal creatures who enjoy the aquatic lakes and rivers. When not in the mountains, they live and hunt in stream beds and in forests. To the folks of Belize, the jaguar is known as the "king" of animals and is spoke about with reverence.

- The **Jaguarundi** is a native to Central America that resides in dense thickets and shrubbery along the edge of forests. While jaguarundis are experts of the ground, they are expert enough to rarely if ever be seen out in the open lands. Even though they are heavily active at night, they still move around a great deal during the daylight hours. They are small cats equipped with a long tail, short legs, and a slender body. Their fur is smooth to the touch.

- The **Margay,** also referred to as the Long Tailed Spotted Cat, looks quite like an Ocelot, but with a smaller body and longer tail and legs. They reside only in forested regions and are accomplished climbers. It devours the insects, frogs, birds, and small monkeys that share the forest.

- **Mountain lions**, also referred to as Belize pumas, are the largest of the Central American felines. They are solitary creatures that avoid human interaction. They cover wide areas of land, from 175-200 miles.

- **Ocelots** are one of the more commonly seen cats of Belize. They reside in the tropical forest areas and stick to the ground, although they are avid climbers. They like to hunt in open spaces during the night and stick to the forested shrubbery during daylight hours.

Other Carnivores

- The **Night-Banded Armadillo** is most active during the day, as it builds burrows and digs for good eats. This animal is swift in movement, despite its clumsy stature.

- **Gray Foxes** are in the woodland regions of Belize, but you can occasionally spot one foraging for insects and fruits without open land. These foxes highly resemble dogs but with bushier tails.

- **Grisons** are known as the Belize Bushdogs. They can be found inhabiting in close range to buildings. They are ferret like in appearance with a distinct white strip. They hunt both during the day and night and often travel in small groups.

- **Neotropical Otters** resides in the lagoons, swamps, streams, and lakes of Belize and all over South America. They are the most common otter species in Mexico. They mainly feast on mollusks, crustaceans, and fish, but also like to enjoy small mammals, birds, and insects.

Omnivores

- The **Cacomistle** looks much like a ring-tailed cat, brown and grey in color. They are distinguished from the tailed cat by its longer tail and pointier ears. They feast on bananas, papayas, figs, and fruits, as well as insects, birds, and mice.

- The **Coatimundi** is also referred to as a "quash" or "Coati" by Belize. They reside in the dense forested areas and feast on fruits, nuts, rodents, snails, and insects. It's easily distinguished by its black and white ringed tail.

- The **Kinkajou**, also known as "night walker" is a nocturnal creature that resides among the upper canopies of the tropical forest. Extremely agile and fast in nature, they can move rapidly among the treetops. They feed on insects and fruits, as well as flower nectar.

- **Spider Monkeys** reside in the forested regions of Belize as well as other areas of Central and South America. They are agile in nature and very powerful amongst the omnivores. They tend to travel in small packs, moving swiftly among the trees. They snack on eggs, seeds, nuts, and insects mainly.

Herbivores

- The **Agouti** is a rodent, medium in size and resembles a guinea pig but with longer and skinnier legs. They feast on fallen nuts and fruits and are wildly attracted to the sound of these items falling to the ground.

- The **Baird's Tapir** is one of the most massive creatures in Belize and is known as "mountain cows," as they can get as big as 800 pounds. They have a thick hide covered with dark brown bristly hair. They are both diurnal and nocturnal and mainly feed on plant matter.

- **Black Howler Monkeys** can certainly be heard before they are seen. They are the largest of the Belize monkeys and feed on flowers, leaves, and fruits.

- The **Paca**, also known as a "gibnut," is a nocturnal rodent. It resides amongst the forest floor and feeds on tubers, fruits, and leaves.

This wildlife section does not even begin to cover the broad array of beautiful species that call Belize its home. There are many kinds of animals, amphibians, reptiles, and more to see in the amazing country of Belize. Learn more later on how you can see these amazing creatures up close!

Vegetation

When it comes to discussing the world of vegetation in Belize, over 60% of the country is covered by luscious forest, with only 20% being covered in cultivated land and human settlements. Belize takes up a good portion of the Mesoamerican Biological Corridor that is found from southern Mexico to the coasts of Panama, making it rich in marine and terrestrial life as well.

While there are many countries that do not take very good care of what they are naturally blessed with, Belize is one that does! They are considered a leader when it comes to the protection of their biodiversity and natural resources they have. There is also about 40% of the country that falls within official protection, which makes it one of the most extensive systems that are terrestrially protected in all of the Americas.

The Infamous Belize Barrier Reef

This renowned barrier reef is made up of a series of coral reefs that straddle the coast of Belize and stretches 175 miles in length It strings from Cancun to the Yucatan Peninsula all the way to Honduras. It is one of the biggest coral reef systems in the world. This is what makes it one of the main reasons that tourists from far and wide venture to Belize, attracting over 260,000 visitors every year.

This reef is not only home to fun activities such as snorkeling and scuba diving (which will be discussed later on), but it is also a vital piece of the fishing industry. The Belize Barrier Reef is home to a very wide variety of animal and plant life, making it one of the most diverse ecosystems in the world as well! This reef is so gigantic in size that only 90% is said to have been discovered, leaving the remaining 10% untouched by human hands. The reef is made up of:

- Hundreds of invertebrate species

- 500+ species of fish

- 35 soft coral species

- 70 hard coral species

Belize is home to a wide array of plant, animal, and marine life that all plays a vital role in the entire ecosystem of the country. Without its network of forests, coastlines, rivers, and low-lying plains, Belize would not be the tourism country it is renowned for today.

Chapter 3
Climate and Weather Conditions

With the wonderful views and wildly elaborate ecosystems that the geography of Belize has to offer visitors, it is also paired with fantastic tropical weather that anyone would enjoy. The tropical climate of Belize does have dominant wet and dry seasons, but it differs from other tropical climates in that the weather patterns vary drastically by region. You can certainly say that the climate is one of the many charms that Belize offers, making people comfortable even in a wildly tropical area.

Average Temperatures

The temperatures of Belize rely heavily on the winds coming from the Caribbean, how close you are to the coastlines, and the elevation in which you are at. The average temperature in Belize along the most coastal regions varies from 75 to 80 degrees Fahrenheit during the months of January through July. Temperatures tend to vary slightly as you venture inland. The coldest temperatures are often found to be in the southern highland plateaus, which is colder all year round.

All seasons in Belize are noticed due to the differences in rainfall and humidity rather than just relying on temperature.

Rainfall

With Belize being a tropical paradise, you must expect a nice amount of rain all year round. The average rainfall varies a lot from the north to the south end of the country. The northern region receives around 53 inches per year, while the southern region receives about 180 inches per year.

In the northern and central areas of Belize during January through May, it tends to see less than 3-4 inches of rain. The drier season is considerably shorter in the southern region. The "dry" season in the southern region only lasts a couple months, usually from February to April.

Hurricanes

Hurricanes have unfortunately been a dramatic part of both key and devastating roles in the history of Belize.

- 1931: an unnamed hurricane wiped out over two-thirds of the buildings in the Belize City and killed more than 1,000 people.

- 1955: Hurricane Janet destroyed the town of Corozal.

- 1961: Hurricane Hatti struck coastal areas of Belize, with four-meter storm tides. With devastation striking Belize City again in under 30 years, this prompted the relocation of the capital to 80 kilometers inland.

- 1978: Hurricane Greta caused $25 million in overall damages along the southern coasts of Belize.

Believe it or not, there was a period that lasted 20 years where Belize was known as a hurricane-free zone. But since there have been hurricanes every few years, ones that completely devastate wherever they land. They have impacted tourism, crippling not only the tourism income but the income Belize receives from importing citrus goods as well.

Climate Description

Enough talk about those pesky hurricanes! Let's look more into the positive attributes that the Belize climate has to offer both citizens and tourists alike!

Since the majority of Belize is made up of gorgeous coastline, the coastal breezes that the sea brings in, along with the tracts of the rainforests and jungles, issues a cooling relief to even the hottest of summer days. If you are looking to escape to somewhere exotic during the bitterly cold winter months, Belize gets a bit cool during its winter, but never extremely cold!

In fact, Belize rarely ever falls below 60 degrees Fahrenheit, while the summers sit at an average of 86 degrees Fahrenheit. The humidity tends to stay consistent at 85%. Isn't this the absolute perfect combination for a weekend getaway or a safe place away from the blustering low temps and breezes of winter back home?!

The "dry season" in Belize occurs between February through May, where there is much less rainfall than throughout the remainder of the year. The "wet season" happens from June to December, where many parts of Belize receive a whopping 150 inches of heavy rain and wild storms. These storms are directly caused by the Caribbean, especially in late afternoons. Thankfully, Belize and neighboring countries are very cooperative when it comes to warning folks about upcoming weather. Their procedures are practiced often and have proven to be highly effective.

Like anywhere in the world, both the wet and dry seasons in Belize have their pros and cons when it comes to traveling. Overall, however, the mild weather that

Belize offers people is one that many can enjoy all year round.

Belize Weather Calendar

No one likes trips ruined thanks to good ole Mother Nature. While it is impossible to accurately predict the weather 100% of the time, here is a good snapshot of Belize weather by each month, so you can plan accordingly!

- **January**: Mild temps and varying rainfall. Start of the dry season. Popular month for visitors. Temperatures range from 70 – 80 degrees.

- **February**: Mild with cooler nights. Very pleasant weather. Temps range from 70-80 degrees.

- **March**: Middle of the dry season, so day and nights typically clear from rainfall. Temperatures vary from 74-83 degrees.

- **April**: The rise of temperatures introduces "Iguana Rains," which are brief, cool showers that appear along the coastlines. Temperatures range from 76-85 degrees.

- **May**: Temperatures continue to rise, with the average being between 79-87 degrees. Rain usually occurs during the morning hours with occasional chances for thunderstorms in the evening.

- **June**: Temperatures average from 82-86 degrees. The breeze from the Caribbean Sea happens more often, which can cause afternoon showers.

- **July**: Temperatures again range from 82-86 degrees. July is quite like June in that rain occurs in the morning. Thunderstorms start becoming more prevalent at night.

- **August**: Drier winds take over the west portion of Belize. The country refers to August as "little dry" since there is a decrease in overall rainfall and a rise in temperatures, averaging between 78-88 degrees. The ultimate average temperature for August is a nice 82 degrees.

- **September**: Belize temperatures begin to change, averages 77-86 degrees. Rainfall chances increase, especially during the morning and at night. Most days are typically filled with warm sunshine.

- **October**: Breezes from the north start to bring in heavier rainfall, with low temperatures of 75 degrees. There are often 2-3 day storms that occur over the Maya Mountains.

- **November:** This month is home to the lowest temperatures in Belize, averaging between 72-79 degrees. There is still often highs in the lower 80's during the sunniest portions of the day. Many climbers find November to be the ideal time to come to Belize.

- **December**: Wet weather arrives in December and the end of the month leaves Belize drier as the wet seasons tone down. The average temperature for December is between 71-80 degrees. This is way better weather to enjoy the holiday season instead of dealing with snowfall! You can even swim during the evening hours here in Belize!

Chapter 4
People, Culture, and Local Dialect

When you officially arrive in the country of Belize, no matter if you are a traveler or if you are planning on staying long term for vacation, the culture and the residing folks of Belize help everyone that steps upon their beautiful country feel comfortable and very welcome. This is another reason it is so darn charming! This welcoming feeling from people around you as you venture through Belize makes it really feel like nowhere else you have ever visited before.

The traditions and customs that the people of Belize celebrate and act upon not only represent them but eight other very diverse cultures. Belize has demonstrated the commitment to preserving the country's unique charms for generations. Their promise to their land and the waters that surround it is what inspires everyone in Belize, even tourists, to achieve a genuine connection to the experiences they encounter while in Belize.

In Belize, you will no doubt find a giant melting pot of colorful people and personalities, which makes the over 321,000 residents of Belize one of the greatest resources regarding tourism! The Belizean people are created from Chinese, Arab, Mennonite, East Indian, Garifuna, Kriol, Mestizo, and Maya. That is quite the collection of human beings!

Among the many cultures of folks that reside in Belize, there are also a number of immigrants from the United States, Europe, and Canada. Many of these folks tend to retire in Belize.

Belize is one of the most peaceful countries in the entire world thanks to this successful blend of people and cultures. It has a worldwide reputation for being one of the friendliest tourist destinations!

Spoken Languages

If you are nervous about not being able to understand folks while you are enjoying the array of cultural diversity in Belize, no worries! Along with the melting pot of cultures comes a broad variety of languages spoken too! Since Belize was formerly the British Honduras, English remains to be the official language of Belize to this day.

Despite this, there are a few other out-of-the-box languages spoken by the people of Belize:

- **Kriol**: This language used to be spelled as "Creole," but with its modernization, it is now spelled "Kriol." Kriol is actually not a different language from English, but rather a distinctive dialect that can be challenging for non-Kriol speakers to understand. In this language, you will often find that traditional Kriol speakers will use "code switch," meaning they speak in the Kriol dialect when they are with family and friends and switch to standard English when in public. About one-third of Belize's population speaks Kriol.

- **Spanish**: Since Belize is in the heart of Central America, it is a country that has been strongly influenced by Spanish. They were especially influenced by the groups of self-styles Mestizos, meaning "mixed race." These folks emigrated during the early 19th century after the civil war in Mexico. You will find that along the Guatemalan and Mexican borders of Belize that these people natively speak Spanish. There are also many Belizeans that speak "kitchen Spanish," which is simply a simplified version of Spanish with the people who us English as their primary language.

- **Mayan**: Our Mayan ancients were responsible for creating the ceremonial sites, palaces, and pyramids that are beautifully sprinkled throughout the Belizean landscape. The Mayan communities are often located within rural areas. Those that speak Mayan also are bilingual in Spanish and/or English as well. The Mayas speak in three dialects:

  - Kekchi

  - Mopan

  - Yucatec

- **Garifuna**: This is a very unique language that is only spoken by about 4% of the Belizean population. Created from an Afro-Caribbean tongue, Garifuna is a mix of indigenous West African and Caribbean languages. It was not truly recognized until 2001 by the United Nations, who finally valued it as a part of the heritage of Belize.

- **German**: The German that is spoken by Belizean people is different from the standard high German known as Hochdeutsch. Belizean German is known as Mennonite or Plautdietsch, which is a low German variety of the Pennsylvania Dutch that is spoken by the Amish communities within the United States. Belize is home to a very established Mennonite community and is made up of several towns and villages. Many folks who speak Belizean German are also bilingual in English.

- **Chinese**: Belize is also home to small but extremely established Chinese communities that are located in the more urbanized areas of the country. The Chinese were brought to Belize as unskilled labor forces but were eventually expanded into more entrepreneurial feats.

- **Arabic**: Although there is not a ton of information regarding the Arabic language dialect in Belize, it hails from Lebanon. Just like the Chinese speaking folks, there are small Arabic-speaking communities that are found in Belize as well.

Many of the Belizean folks are very religious, with the majority of Belize's population strongly following the Roman Catholic faith. But since Belize was once strongly under British rule, there are many members that follow Anglican and other varieties of Protestant Christianity. Among the larger majorities of religion, there is a minority of German-Swiss Mennonites that follow their own faith.

When you visit Belize, you will often hear more familiar words than you would think. In fact, Belize is the only country that has English as its main native language in the entirety of Central America. When you hear conversations spouting from both the mouths of Belizean citizens and seasoned tourists, you will find the conversations surprisingly relaxed, even from the citizens that seem to have an uptight persona. Even though you will hear our words that are a bit shorter, you will be able to easily understand everything that is said, even when it comes to learning phrases Belizeans teach you that you otherwise did not know.

One of the cool things about the Belize is that even the English language has wildly diversity throughout. From English to German to Mandarin, Belize has some of the most intriguing arrays of dialects when it comes to its language.

You will hear many ways that common phrases are said as you journey through the areas of Belize. For example, here are a few ways you may hear the phrase "good morning":

- *"Buenos dias"* – Spanish

- *"Buiti Binafi"* – Garifuna

- *"Gud Mawnin"* – Kriol

Belizean Holidays

Belize is widely renowned for its plethora of holidays, especially since the country heavily promotes relaxation and leisure.

- National Heroes and Benefactors Day

- Sovereign's Day

- St. George's Caye Day

- Pan American Day

- Garifuna Settlement Day

Chapter 5
Major Cities

When potential visitors of Belize begin to search about the places that make up this wonderful and diverse country, they will be surprised that Belize, even though it comes off as a strictly tropical area, there are very populated and urban cities that counteract the gorgeous and unpopulated coastlines. This chapter we will look at the top 10 largest cities in the country of Belize.

Belize City

Belize City is the biggest city of Belize with a population of 57,000+. This city was once the capital of this country when it was once the former British Honduras. It is located near the opening of Haulover Creek, which is a branch of the immense Belize River.

Belize City is Belize's financial and industrial hub and principal port. There are hundreds of cruise ships that drop anchors at its port each year that are tendered by local citizens. Belize City was almost completely destroyed by Hurricane Hattie in 1961, which is what prompted the relocation of the capital in 1970, which is now Belmopan.

This city is split into two portions; The Northside, that is bordered by Haulover Creek and ends within the area of Fort George. And the Southside, that goes to the outskirts of Belize City and through the Port area, which includes downtown.

The culture of Belize City is much like the other capital cities with the Caribbean. The hustle and bustle of the city is one that even foreigners would enjoy getting used to. There are museums, galleries, and festivals throughout the year. The majority of Belize City citizens work within the downtown region since the city is home to many major banks, insurance centers, and marketplaces. This city is also the hub for road, sea, and international travel.

San Ignacio

San Ignacio is a town in western Belize that is an important cultural and economic hub, located in the heart of the Cayo District. The city has a very diverse population of people, making it the largest settlement in the Cayo District.

San Ignacio used to be known as El Cayo, named by the Spanish. It is located on the banks of the Macal River, 60+ miles west of Belize City. It is 2 ½ square miles in size. The population of this town is mainly made up of Kriol and Mestizo.

During the recent years, San Ignacio has managed to take in the once separated village of Santa Elena. This is what makes this town the second largest urban region in Belize. The two towns are connected simply by a suspension bridge across the Macal River. They are referred to by Belizean citizens as "Twin Towns."

Orange Walk Town

Orange Walk Town is the capital of the Orange Walk District, located on the left bank of the New River. It has a population of 13,400 people and is the 4th largest town in Belize.

When the days of the Mayans were in play, this town was known as Holpatin. It is the home to the biggest Maya temple that was built during the pre-classic period during the 1500's.

Orange Walk Town is very populated by Indians, Taiwanese, Chinese, Mennonites, Kriols, and Mayas. There is a very prominent Roman Catholic presence in this town as well.

Belmopan

Belmopan is the current capital city of Belize. It is populated by 16,500 people and is actually the smallest of all the capital cities in the continental Americas. It was founded in 1970 and is one of the newest national capital cities worldwide. Ever since 2000, Belmopan has been one of only two settlements in the country of Belize to hold official city status.

Located in the Cayo District, Belmopan is 249 feet above sea level and constructed right east of the Belize River, only a few miles inland from the former capital of Belize City.

The layout of the city centers directly around Ring Road, which is about 4 kilometers in circumference. Many governmental buildings are centered around Ring Road. The buildings were designed with the idea of ventilation in mind to help accommodate for the climate.

There is a wide variety of ethnicities that make up Belmopan, from Mestizo to Chinese. There are many noteworthy events that occur in Belize's capital throughout the year.

Dangriga

Known previously as Stann Creek Town, Dangriga is located in southern Belize along with coast of the Caribbean along the mouth of the North Stann Creek River. Dangriga is the capital of the Stann Creek District and is served strongly by the Dangriga Airport.

This city is also referred to as "the culture capital of Belize" thanks to its influence of punta music and forms of Garifuna culture. It happens to be the largest settlement in southern Belize. Dangriga's population is made up of Mestizos, Kriols, and Garinagu with a population of less than 9,000.

Home to Garifuna, which is an ethnic group made up of native Caribs and slaves that shipwrecked onto Belizean shores, they have adopted the Carib language but kept the African music and other traditions.

Corozal Town

Corozal Town is the capital of Corozal District that is located just 9 miles from the Mexico border. The population of this town is less than 10,000. It was just a private estate before it molded into the town it is today in the 1840's. It was settled by Maya Mestizo refugees that survived during the Caste War of Yucatan. The majority of the town was built over the ancient Maya city of Santa Rita.

Corozal Town was one of the worst damaged areas during Hurricane Janet in 1955 but thanks to its dedicated citizens, was built quickly after the incident.

San Pedro Town

San Pedro Town is in the southern portion of the Belizean island of Ambergris Caye. The population is more than the previously discussed towns, at about 16,500, making it the second largest town in the Belize Rural South District. It is also referred to Belizeans as "the sleepy fishing village," the status being granted in 1984.

Those that inhabit San Pedro Town are known as San Pedranos, and they mainly speak Spanish and English. The town is said to be the inspiration for the song "La Isla Bonita." Over the last couple centuries, San Pedro Town has become a wildly popular tourist destination. It is made up of protected areas like Shark Ray Alley, Hol Chan Marine Reserve, and Bacalarchico (to be discussed later on!)

One of Belize's most prized possessions is in San Pedro Town, being the Belize Barrier Reef. It is the second largest barrier reef in the world, with the first being the Great Barrier Reef. The reef is home to a wide array of species. This means that scuba diving is a very popular activity, which is why so many tourists visit this town.

Benque Viejo del Carmen

This town is the westernmost of all in Belize, sitting near the border of Guatemala. The Mopan River runs along the northern and western borders of this town.

Thanks to the Maya, Benque was settled along the Mopan River in 1865. Benque has been a popular place where both merchants and tourists cross Melchor to purchase beautiful Maya textiles. The Guatemalan youth cross this border often to receive secondary education in the form of English. Benque is home to annual fiestas, the Belize Premier Football League team, educational experiences, and a variety of supermarkets.

Punta Gorda

Locally referred to as "P.G.", Punta Gorda is the capital as well as the largest town in the Toledo District, located in southern Belize. With a population of 5,000, Punta Gorda is the most sizeable town in the southernmost nation. Even though the town's name is Spanish oriented, those that reside here are mainly English and Kriol speaking.

This town is a fishing and seaport town directly on the Caribbean Sea. It used to be just a tiny fishing village until it was settled by Garifuna emigrants who came from Honduras in 1823. Those that are Garifuna call the town "Peini."

Punta Gorda is the main place for transportation for those that head and visit the Toledo District. There is a small airport that serves flights from Maya Island Air and Tropic Air. There are tons of hotels with amazing ocean views that line the Punta Gorda streets, which is why it is such a tourist attraction. The town is a direct gateway to jungle accommodations, such as the Cotton Tree Lodge and Hickatee Cottages.

Punta Gorda is responsible for hosting the Toledo Cacao Festival, which celebrates the ancient and modern-day connections with chocolate and cacao.

Placencia

Placencia is a tiny town located within the Stann Creek District of Belize. This village is a place that 1,500+ people call home. The Peninsula is located on the eastern side of the town, with beautiful white beaches and mangroves sprinkling the area. There are prominent settlements along the North and South peninsulas, such as Maya Beach Village, Garifuna Village, and Placencia Village.

Chapter 6
Renowned Locations

One of the most exciting aspects about planning any kind of get away from the everyday stress is searching for intriguing, entertaining, and thrilling things to do while you are visiting exotic and out of this world locations!

While there are some destinations in the world that are far from ideal for most of the year, Belize is one of the dreamiest places to head to when you need to fulfill your hope of beauty within the hustle and bustle of everyday life. Belize is a country where you hardly have to be concerned about the weather, as well as being bored and not finding things to do! There are a plethora of unique experiences and places in Belize that are waiting for you to feast your eyes on!

Tourist Attractions

Picture yourself among exotic wildlife, in cave formation, swimming among coral reefs and walking along tropical beaches as you feast your eyes on the knowledge of these amazing destinations within Belize.

Belize Zoo

Located 30 miles from Belize City, this zoo is not only the finest zoos in the Americas, but it is one of the most unique in the entire world. It is set right within the natural forest, making it no ordinary zoo. Animal lovers will truly enjoy their time being engulfed among the large, realistic enclosures as they peer at the rescued native animals of Belize. The Belize Zoo is also referred to "best little zoo in the world." If that's not a reason to visit, I don't know what is!

Actun Tunichil Muknal

Near San Ignacio, the Actun is a cave located in the depths of the Tapir Mountain Nature Reserve.

Discovered in 1992, this attraction has been featured on the film *"Journey Through the Underworld"* that was created by National Geographic. It used to be a sacred site for the Mayans, which is why the cave has stoneware, ceramics, pottery, and sacrificial remains that cover the limestone crystals, which are created by the cave's natural processes.

Xunantunich

The Maya ruins of Xunantunich are upon the very top of the ridge near San Ignacio, above the Mopan River. From here you can see the Guatemala border. The majority of the structures date clear back to 200-900 B.C. It consists of six plazas that are surrounded by 26 palaces and temples.

Cockscomb Basin Wildlife Sanctuary

This sanctuary is one of the largest destinations in Belize, as well as one of the most protected. Also known as the Jaguar Reserve, it was founded in 1990, making it the first sanctuary that homed the jaguar. The sanctuary houses only about 60 of Belize's 700 big cats, which makes the chance of actually seeing one for yourself slim. Nonetheless, this is an ideal location to visit to see exotic birds and other wildlife. The system of trails is one of the best in all of Belize's protected areas.

San Pedro Town

Located on Ambergris Caye, one of the biggest islands in the northern water of Belize, San Pedro town is one of the hottest tourist location in all of Belize. With the lack of city traffic and large hotels, visitors find this town to be laid back, where you can get to most in-town locations by simply walking. This is also a great place to stay during your time in Belize, thanks to quality hotels and the resorts that line the islands.

Lamanai

This once large Maya city is located in the northern part of Belize where visitors and citizens alike can easily view much if the ancient ruins. There has been much archaeological work done to restore the structures. It was once occupied by the Maya, named from the Spanish-derived word "Lamanai," which means "submerged crocodile." It is one of the few Mayan sites that has managed to retain its original namesake.

Hopkins

Located south of Dangriga, Hopkins is a small village that stretches along the bay and is widely known as the center of culture within the Garifuna population of Belize. The town is well-known for hosting its very own national holiday, known as Hopkins Day. The celebration welcomes citizens and tourists alike to celebrate Garifuna Independence Day with drum ceremonies that last all day into the wee hours of the night. This village is an amazing place to learn about the unique aspects of the Garifuna culture.

Placencia

Located in the southern portion of Belize, Placencia is a very popular peninsula that is inhabited by beaches and offshore coral cayes. The eastern side of this peninsula is sprinkled with very white and beachy sands, with the western side is bounded by a narrow bay. The gorgeous beaches paired with the cheap accommodations make this a great place to stay while in Belize.

Caracol

Sitting 500 meters above sea level, Caracol is one of the biggest Mayan sites within Belize, which sits high among the Vaca Plateau. It once covers 168 square miles back when the ancient Mayans ruled Belize. It has been estimated that during its peak in 650 A.D., the population was 150,000, which is twice as much as Belize City today!

The Canaa is the biggest pyramid in Caracol is 143 feet high, which makes it the tallest man-made structure in Belize.

Caye Caulker

Located on a small coral island in the Caribbean Sea, Caye Caulker is easily accessible by a small place or water taxi. The island has become a quite popularized Belize attraction, especially for backpacking tourists. Thanks to its low prices, abundant bars, and restaurants, as well as the calm, laid-back vibe, it makes this island an amazing place to stay during your time in Belize. Caulker is lined with many awesome walking paths that only take 20-30 minutes to walk, or you can rent bicycles or golf carts as well.

Great Blue Hole

If you are an avid diver, you need to put the Great Blue Hole down on your list of "must-do's" while you are in Belize. It is known as the most popular diving location in Belize, offering intriguing limestone formations and observations that line the walls. It is a sinkhole that is near the Lighthouse Reef, which is why it creates an almost perfect circle of beautifully deep blue waters. The water becomes even prettier once you engulf yourself into it, as you can see bizarre stalactites becoming more complex and intense in nature.

Belize Barrier Reef

190 miles in length, the Belize Barrier Reef is the second biggest coral reef system in the world. It is no wonder that it's among Belize's top tourist attractions, making it popular for snorkeling and scuba diving. Much of the reef is protected by the Belize Barrier Reef Reserve System, with 3 atolls, 450 cayes, and 7 marine reserves protected vigorously. This reef is home to the Great Blue Hole, which is a widely renowned diving location.

Sarteneja

If you are looking for a picturesque and quaint location while in Belize, this location of the Shipstern Peninsula within the Corozal District fulfills this wonderfully. What makes this destination super unique is the Mestizo and Creole communities that sit among the tropical bay. The two main industries are pineapple farming and lobster fishing, with a significant source of income coming from tourism.

Shipstern Wildlife Reserve

Known as one of the top attractions in all of Belize, this reserve is made up of 31 miles of beautiful tropical forestry. It is owned and operated by organizations that are non-governmental. Here you will feast your eyes upon a grand array of out of this world vegetation.

Mayflower Bacowina National Park

If you are one that enjoys venturing off the beaten track, then add this national park to your list of Belizean places. Located in the Stann Creek District, it offers amazing views of Maya sites, swimming holes, trails, waterfalls, and the Maya Mountains. There are around 200 species of birds as well as an array of wildlife spotted at this park. You can also experience a lengthy zip-line course within the Mayflower.

Chiquibul Cave System

This is the longest network of caves within all of Central America and even includes the largest cave room known in the entire Western hemisphere. They have been created by the Chiquibul River, which has carved them out over time. They originated in the Maya Mountains and submerged underground and re-emerged in Guatemala.

Shark Ray Alley

Located in the Hol Chan Marine Reserve, Shark Ray Alley is one of the most popular and visited diving and snorkeling sites in Belize. While it may sound pretty intimidating to nurse stingrays and sharks, they are harmless and used to the human attention. You can feed and pet them! Isn't that cool?! You will be taken away by the huge schools of barracuda, snappers, groupers, and jacks that can be seen swimming in a short distance away.

Chapter 7
Places to Stay and Transportation

No great vacation to a faraway destination is complete without a place to rest your head to recharge for another day of adventure! In this chapter, you will find must-stay locations as well as ways to get around Belize so that you can see the most of this charming country and all that makes it amazing in the time you have to spend there.

Ambergris Caye

This is the biggest of the islands that make up the outskirts of Belize. This is a tropical place where your exotic day-dreams could easily come true. With flip-flops and shorts being the dress code and golf carts being the main form of transportation, you could spend hours on the white sandy beaches as a great activity and be fulfilled. Ambergris Caye is an ultimate spot to visit while in Belize since it presents itself as its very own Caribbean getaway, thanks to its fabulous dining experiences, promoting of relaxation, and classic beaches.

- **Azul Resort** is made up of two white villas that are stretched along the beach, equipped with a private dock and pool.

- **Cayo Espanto** is a luxury resort that is tucked right behind San Pedro Town. It has crystal clear waters that contain a nice handful of villas that are phenomenal in sight.

- **El Secreto** is a new resort that is within Ambergris Caye. It is equipped with a spa, exclusive restaurant, pool, and much more!

- **Mata Chica Resort and Spa** is right north of the Azul Resort and is made up of a nice collection of roofed cabanas that are sprinkled with trees that harbor tropical fruit. You can easily be whisked away by the fleet of boats that Mata Chica has to offer, along with an attentive staff.

- **Gaia River Lodge** is the sister resort of the Mata Chica Resort and has a pool to die for. It is made up of a jungle-inspired lodge, which makes it a gorgeously exotic resort to add to your list.

- **The Phoenix** is the closest to a town than any of the others in Ambergris Caye, located right on the end of Front Street in San Pedro. Equipped with a giant modernized kitchen and massive balconies overlooking a huge pool, you will enjoy not only these sights but the accommodations of a gym and an exclusive restaurant as well.

- The **Victoria House Resort** is gorgeous, as it is inspired by colonial plantations. Located just 2 miles south of San Pedro, it spans over a huge and very green in color property, which is rare to see in Belize. It harbors a civilized beach bar and spa, which is one of the biggest on the entire island.

Cayo District

- The **Blancaneux Resort** is a refurbished place that is a hotspot for celebrities since its owned by Francis Coppola. Since the 1980's, this once abandoned family retreat has been remodeled to mirror the country of Belize with indoor waterfalls, mountains, wildlife, and jungle scenery. If this wasn't enough, the entire resort is filled with photos that frame the history of Belize.

- The **Chaa Creek** is amongst the greens of the jungle. If you decide to stay here, you will also be presented with complimentary tours! The art that the rooms exhibit was hand-picked by the owners. The bar is equipped with real wood directly from the jungles of Belize. You will literally be called from breakfast to see a troop of monkeys flying through the trees.

- The **Ka'ana Resort** is located in the heart of the jungle and all the activities that go on. From the caves to the Mayan inspired sites, you can spend literal days exploring the land of Belize. If comfort is on your list of must-needs for where you are staying, this hotel lines its beds with Egyptian cotton sheets and are equipped with yoga mats for exercise and prayer schedules. Their restaurant is to die for as well, with innovative and fresh Belizean cuisine.

Placencia

- The **Turtle Inn Resort** is a luxurious resort in Placencia. One of the main attractions of this place is that each room is equipped with conch shell phones. Request a wake-up call and hear through one of these!

Caye Caulker

Caye Caulker is not only beautiful but a great place to stay when you are on a budget and still want to see the shores of Belize. There is an array of restaurants and bars that attract tourists year-round. You can easily access the island by water taxi or place. While this is not the most ideal place for sight-seeing, it is amazing if you wish to simply relax and hang out in the wonderful Belizean weather away from the everyday.

Belize City

Located on the peninsula at the mouth of Haulover Creek, Belize City is one of the main transportation hubs in Belize. While many tourists and short-comers spend very little time among the streets of Belize City, it is widely known for its culture and number of tourist attractions. There are also many relatively cheap places to stay within the city limits of this town as well.

Tobacco Caye

Located at the northern end of the South Water Caye Marine Reserve, Tobacco Caye is a relatively small island that is only 10 miles from Dangriga. Those that visit the island are allowed to choose from 6 lodges that promote relaxation and rest. Because of its location in a marine reserve, it is an excellent destination for shore diving. This is one of the reasons that it comes up on many snorkel, scuba diving, and backpacker enthusiast's radars.

San Ignacio

San Ignacio is a very relaxed and friendly city that is located 22 miles from Belmopan. It offers a plethora of inexpensive hotels, bus connections, yummy foods and a great climate. This town is surrounded by beautiful forested hills and rivers, which makes it ideal for those that have made it a priority to explore the Mayan ruins. San Ignacio also serves as a transit town if you are in route to Guatemala, which is why it is commonly referred to by the locals as Cayo. This word in the Spanish language is used to describe offshore islands and locations.

Getting Around in Belize

A grand part of the Belizean adventure is getting around the country! No worries, transportation is easy and all part of the authenticity of Belize. The most ideal ways to get around the country are by plane, water taxi, or car. But there are more adventurous ways as well, such as bike, golf cart, or horseback.

Since attractions among the mainlands of Belize are quite spread out, Belize is equipped with a plethora of commuter buses that will transport you to the most popular and renowned things to do while in Belize.

Water Taxi

Water taxis typically operate around Caye Caulker, Ambergris Caye, and Belize City. The cays and small atolls are not visited as frequently by tourists, which is why water taxis are often required. There are many of these taxi services, such as the San Pedro Belize Express, which operates shuttle services daily between the above locations. It is very inexpensive as well, with one-way tickets costing just $15 to $20.

Taxi

Taxis are easy to come by as well as flag down in Ambergris Caye, Belize City, and San Pedro. The fares are fairly cheap at $6 to $14. Be aware, however, that many taxis are not equipped with a fixed meter that you can consistently look at. Make sure to agree on a price with the driver of the taxi.

In Caye Caulker, you can be chauffeured by golf carts instead of taxis. You can also rent golf carts at daily and weekly fees.

Car

Belize is made up of four primary roads:

- Northern

- Western

- Southern

- Hummingbird

All of these highways are very easy to drive on and navigate through, which makes driving one of the most ideal modes of transportation. This is especially true if you are planning to visit the outlying Mayan sites. Rental cars are easily accessible, especially by the major airports. But you will be unable to rent a car in Belize if you fail to acquire an international driving permit. If you are unable to get one of these, you should consider renting a four-wheel drive vehicle, as some roads that lead to places like the Mayan ruins are rustic. In rainy weather, you do not want to get a rental car stuck in these conditions, making a four-wheeler way easier to operate.

Bus

There are many bussing companies among all areas of Belize, especially along the main highways. But there is no standard bus system within Belize City. The price to take a bus vary on the distance you plan to travel, as well as the company and kind of service you use. One of the major companies, Autotransportes De Oriente (ADO) provides people with transportation from Belize City to places like Orange Walk Town and Corozal, located in northern Belize. They can also take you to the nearby Mexican destination, such as Playa del Carmen and Cancun.

Another reputable bus service is James Bus, which offers transportation daily between Dangriga, Punta Gorda, and Belize City.

Plane

A very hassle-free way to travel all around the country of Belize is by commuter airlines. Maya Island Air and Tropic Air offer transport daily to the Belize City Municipal Airport and the Philip S.W. Goldson International Airport, which can then take you to the most popular of Belizean destinations. Prices directly rely on the season you are in Belize, the airline you choose, and the route you are taking.

Chapter 8
Additional Information

There are many factors that travelers fail to consider when planning a vacation away from the everyday. This chapter will help to ensure you get the most out of your time in Belize without any of those pesky hassles.

Preparing to Head to Belize

Here are the top tips to consider when it comes to planning all aspects of your Belizean getaway!

Travel documents

Most folks are not required to obtain visas before they enter Belize. All you will need is a passport that has been valid for longer than 6 months.

Another consideration to think about is the airport departure tax and exit fees.

Choosing destinations

Belize might be small in size but it has a plethora of locations and activities to offer. To get the most out of your Belizean experience, you need to consider what sort of locations you wish to visit and see, as well as what seasons are best to experience these destinations.

To plan the best Belize vacation possible, you need to be able to spend your time wisely, since getaway time goes way faster than time spent hating your job at the office. Research the top things to do in Belize, how to make the most of your week, and how to make the most from the entirety of your Belizean stay!

Choosing the Right Modes of Transportation

Along with choosing locations in Belize, you need to choose and budget transportation expenses to ensure you can get around the country with ease.

Packing for Belize

Here is a list of Belize travel essentials to ensure you are comfortable with your adventures: http://www.belizeadventure.ca/travel-tips/packing-list/

Know the Languages

Thankfully, you do not need to spend an extensive amount of time when it comes to becoming seasoned with the language of Belize to understand it since English is the main dialect. But if you plan to venture close to the borders of Mexico or Guatemala, you may need to brush up on your Spanish a bit. Regardless of ethnicity, the majority of Belizeans speak English based Kriol, so it will be quite easy to understand what the residents are saying to you.

Know Methods of Payment

The Belizean dollar is the most standard currency, but almost every location as you venture through Belize do accept the United States dollar. The rate of exchange is BZ$2.oo to US$1.00. Exchanges of money can easily be done at a few businesses, hotels, and banks. Ensure you carry various forms of currency with you as you travel, from traveler's checks, debit or credit cards, or cash. And always carry more than one card, in the case you lose it or it becomes lost, damaged, or stolen.

Things Newbies Should Know about Belize

- Placencia is the only location that you are allowed to drink water right from the tap since there is an underwater spring that lies below the town. Remember to consume water anywhere else in Belize.

- Belize is not somewhere that you have to worry about high crime rates, even on the road. Things you need to consider when traveling is that:

  - The sun sets early

  - Do not drive at night in Belize if it's your first time

  - Know where checkpoints are located

  - Know where speed humps are

- The Belizean sun rises at 5:30 A.M. all year round and set at around 6:00 P.M. Belize loves its happy hours, which tend to happen right as the sun sets.

- In San Pedro, Caye Caulker, and Placencia, there are no sidewalks along the main roads, so watch yourself along these as you tread on them by foot.

- You will almost immediately notice that there are dogs everywhere in Belize. The Belizeans refer to them as "beach dogs." No worries, they will rarely if ever hurt you.

- Tipping at restaurants, of course, is appreciated. But you do not need to tip as much as say, the United States, which is 10%.

- In Belize, almost everything is capable of being delivered if you simply ask.

- You really don't need a car when traveling on Belize, especially if you are staying near town. You can easily walk to everything and experience tours that can pick you up and take you to popular destinations.

- While the beaches of Belize are amazing to experience, the Cayes are the best places to go! Instead of being concerned about the seagrass and similar items on the beach, rent a boat to take out near the islands! I highly recommend boating to the Mesoamerican Barrier Reef. Once you become seasoned to the islands of Belize, your entire picture of a happy scenery to daydream of will be totally remolded.

- If you have a hankering for your taste buds to experience some exotic brews, then Belize is a country you certainly will not want to miss out on. There is a small choice of beers within the Caribbean. But the Belize Brewing Company has totally taken over the market with their Belikin beers, stouts, and Lighthouse beer, along with other seasonal varieties. Brews that are made internationally are challenging to find, so enjoy them while you can!

- Even though history class makes us perceive that the Mayan no longer exist, they are still alive and well in Belize, as they make up 10% of the population. The word Belize is actually made from Belikin, which is Mayan for "Land Facing the Sea."

- Obviously, there are tons of amazing things about Belize, but the invisible sandflies are critters that are not so pleasant. Ensure that you pack clothes with sleeves for when the wind stops blowing outside, as the sandflies will swarm everywhere by the hundreds.

- Belize is one of the only places in the world that visitors can experience five ecosystems within a two-hour drive from one another. You will see mangroves, oceans, rivers, jungles, and savannahs. This is what makes Belize the capital of eco-tourism within the Central Americas.

- The activity known as cave tubing can only be experienced in Belize.

- The world's most narrow street is in Placencia. It is only 4 feet and connects a variety of bars, restaurants, and coffee shops. It extends 16 miles long.

- Belize is the only country in Central America to have the lowest density in population. Despite being the size of Massachusetts, it can feel roomy at only 35 people per square mile. Even during popular tourist seasons, you will not have to fight for space on the beach. This is what makes Belize a truly relaxing country to get away from the hustle and bustle of the everyday.

- If you are overly pleased by your temporary stay in Belize, why not make it more permanent? Buying property in this country is actually affordable, believe it or not. It is easy to locate an island home for under $50,000 U.S. dollars!

- Even though Belize is an independent nation, you will more than likely witness the colonial English roots coming out! The Queen visits the shores of Belize quite often.

- There are over 500 types of birds within Belize, if not more. So, for the avid bird watcher, venturing to Belize is a must-do that should be on the bucket list of destinations.

- If you wish to travel somewhere where you can easily avoid people, then Belize is the place for you.

- You can eat varieties of meat that are unable to be transported to consume anywhere else in the world! While many outsiders believe that Belizeans only consume items such as shrimp, fish, and lobster 24/7, the Belize's culinary fame is actually the rodent. Gibnut is like chicken to Belize, but twice as yummy and not served anywhere else.

- Thanks to Belize's easy-going weather, it is easy to just pack one suitcase full of gear on your Belizean travels.

- The Belize motto is, *"Under the shade, we flourish."* How relaxed is that?

- The mahogany tree heritage that has been long-standing has morphed the economy in Belize to one that is based on tourism. This means that these beautiful trees no longer have to be sacrificed for Belize to grow economically.

- If you ever have to deal with the court system in any way, you will soon feel like you are in London. Why? Because Belize adopted the United Kingdom's legality system, clear down to the courtroom appearances.

- Expect to pay around BZ$8.00 for quick meals at a local restaurant and around BZ$30-$40 for a nice meal with drinks. Snack and fruits here are wildly cheap since many of the food sold is local. But expect to pay around 30% higher around the more touristy places, especially in or near the Cayes.

- Most accommodations around Belize (unless you are staying at extravagant hotels) are cheap, around BZ$30.00 per night. Private rooms cost between BZ$70-$100. There is also Airbnb here as well, with entire homes available for rent from BZ$50-$150 per night.

- Even though the activities and sights to see in Belize are amazing, there is no need to pay an extensive price to experience the country. Mayan ruins and national parks cost around BZ$16-$20, with full day trips costing BZ$200.00. If you are into sea kayaking, then you can experience it for just BZ$60.00!

- The suggested budget for a day in Belize is 100BZ /50USD. This is assuming you plan to stay in a hotel, cook a majority of your own meals, eat out on occasion, and use local ways of transportation. Here are some ways to help you save money while visiting Belize:

  - Travel during off-peak times, between October through April.

  - Camping can save you bunches on accommodation costs.

  - Using public transportation systems will help you save money and get you to more popularized areas.

- Hitchhiking is a common occurrence among the locals. If you are brave enough to venture into other people's vehicles, this can be a very unique way to experience Belize from a local's point of view.

- Combine trips! There are many tour operators that combine excursions, which is a great way to save on transfers to each individual tourist destination.

- Many of the bars have happy hours during the late afternoons and offer 2 for the price of one drinks.

- Instead of buying all your consumables at supermarkets, bring your own food. This will help you to save both time and money.

- If you really plan ahead, you can easily find places to couch-surf. Places like Belize that have warm locals host tourists and visitors from all over the world. You won't have to pay for a place to stay, but you will have your very own local host who can direct and even show you the best place to go!

Belize is only a short venture away! From the laid-back nature of the Belize culture to the exotic beachy feel with an array of wildlife, the views, sights, sounds, and smells of the entire country of Belize will fill you with the essence of a getaway that you will never want to leave.

There is something for everyone in the country of Belize, whether you are a history buff, an adventure junkie, or someone that loves experiencing all of the senses of an exotic but not so far away land.

After your visit to Belize, you can rest assured that you will never daydream the same ever again, as you imagine your journey along the coastlines, diving into the crystal clear water of the Belize and engulfing yourself in the diverse cultures that will forever whisk you away from the everyday.

Conclusion

Congratulations on successfully journeying through *Belize: The Official Travel Guide*!

I hope that the chapters of this book were able to give you a clear picture of what to expect if you ever venture to the country of Belize. Stunning in nature, this small piece of heaven on Earth has a way of whisking you away from all your troubles.

If you are searching for a one-stop destination for amazing views of the ocean to an impressive array of ancient attractions, Belize must be written on your bucket list of "must-visit" places. You only live once, right?

This book was written in hopes that you as a reader would feel destined to visit Belize for yourself and to make it a priority to see all the fantastic and out-of-this-world beachy views! I hope that this book provided you with all the valuable information and tools you need to make the most out of your next potential vacation to the shores of Belize.

If you found this book to be valuable and entertaining in any way, before you hop on a plane to Belize, please take a moment to stop by Amazon and leave a review of your thoughts of *Belize: The Official Travel Guide*! It's sure appreciated!

Description

If you are troubled in your search for a wild place on Earth to visit that is just a hop, skip, and a jump away, perhaps it is time to give the shores of Belize a chance!

With the varieties of cultures embedded in this small but big in attractions country, Belize is your one-stop destination for ocean views and activities, great food, cultured dancing, beautiful sunsets, and much, *much* more! Previous Belize travelers have described this gorgeous country to be a *"real treasure of a trip."*

While Belize has been beyond blessed by Mother Nature, the elements that make this country unlike any others you will visit is the rainbow of people from arrays of cultures that come together and create the diverse society that is unified and highly likable!

It is no doubt that Belize is its very own paradise, one that words fail to describe. Thank goodness this book is not only packed with tons of valuable information about Belize, but it is loaded with plenty of amazing pictures for you to feast your eyes on.

What are you waiting for? The endless ocean skylines, the deliciously mixed cuisine and the plethora of activities at Belize are waiting for you to experience them for yourself!

85807176R00053

Made in the USA
Lexington, KY
04 April 2018